BOOK

GW00691581

Together in **Drum Trainer Book 2** we will steadily progress your training to **grade level.**

This requires a number of **playing styles** so we have taken different aspects of **technique** and **rudiments** and placed them in specially-written songs.

This will help you build a better picture and understanding of **practical playing** and **greater performance.**

THE CHALLENGE IS ON!

REMEMBER

1. If you do not understand anything, ask your coach (Teacher).
2. Make sure you do **20 minutes** Home Training every day.
3. Get your parents to sign your training schedule, because the points you get all go towards your final awards.
4. Sometimes Home Training is hard but NEVER let it beat you!

STICK AT IT, WORK HARD, HAVE FUN, YOU WILL BE THE BEST!!!

Below you will find **6 common rudiments** to be played on a **snare drum**. As you get more comfortable with **playing patterns**, you will be able to transfer these exercises onto different parts of the drum kit. There are many different **rudiments** to study but the following are a **good starting point**.

Remember!
Start off **slowly** then build up speed once the **technique** has been **mastered**.

Set the metronome to: ♩ = **80 bpm**

1 Single strokes.

R L R L R L R L R L R L R L R L

2 Double strokes.

R R L L R R L L R R L L R R L L

3 Triplet.

R L R L R L R L R L R L

4 Triplet 6.

R L L R L L R L L R L L

5 Paradiddle.

R L R R L R L L R L R R L R L L

6 flam.

R L   L R   R L   L R

Below you will find **1 bar rhythms** repeated. There are **6 training patterns** to study. **Exercises 7 and 10** are used in **'pop style'** on Page 6.

When you have mastered the **pop song** on page 6 use it as a **backing track** to improvise with patterns **8, 9, 11 and 12.**

Set the metronome to: ♩ = 80 bpm

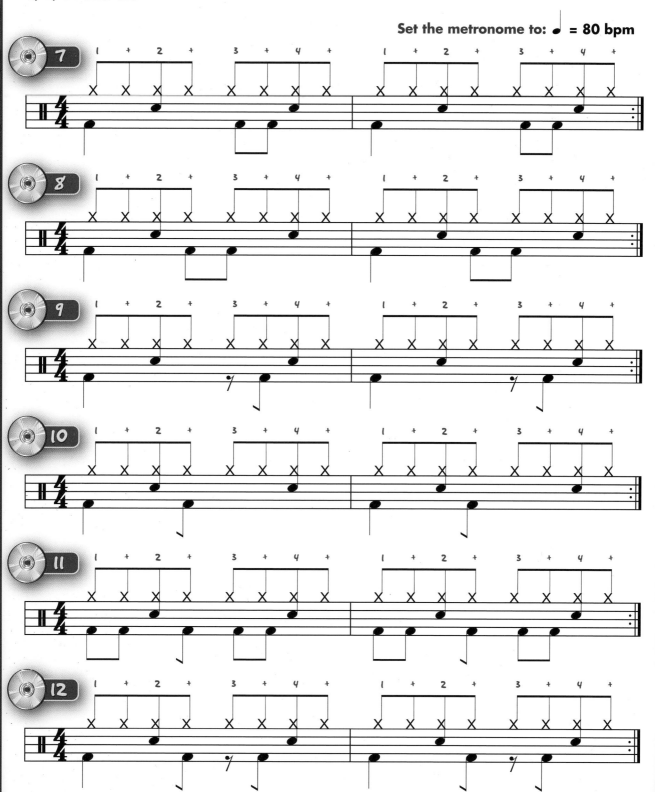

Pop Sense.

SONG

13 + 14

Set the metronome to: ♩ = 90 bpm

Exercises 15, 16 & 17 are still **1 bar rhythms** and **exercises 18, 19 & 20** are **2 bar rhythms.**

To play in the style of **punk** incorporates **quick playing** and **good coordination.** Again, don't start off too fast whilst you're learning the exercises otherwise bad technique will **break down the flow.**

Exercises 19 and 20 are commonly used in **punk tracks** you may hear on the radio.

Set the metronome to: ♩ = **90 bpm**

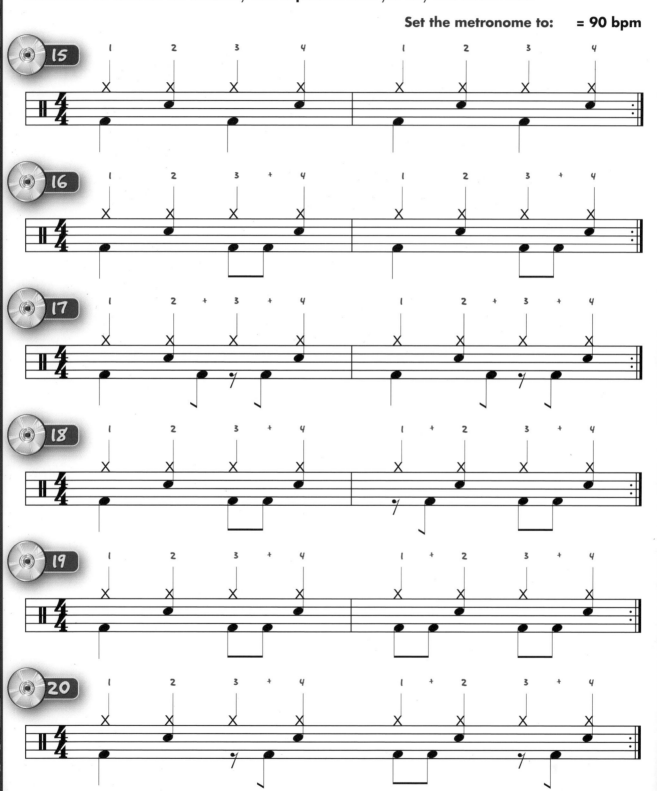

Punk U like.

Session 13

21 + 22

Set the metronome to: ♩ = 90 bpm

metronome **90** setting

Sixteenth Note Rhythms.

Here we look at **16th notes**. A good way to count the **rhythm** is to think of **"Co - ca - Co - la"**.

From **exercises 23 – 27** the top line remains the same. This is to help you **concentrate** on keeping a **solid pulse** with **both hands** and improve your co-ordination with the **bass pedal.**

Session 14

Co - ca - Co - la

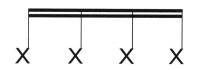

Set the metronome to: ♩ = 60 bpm

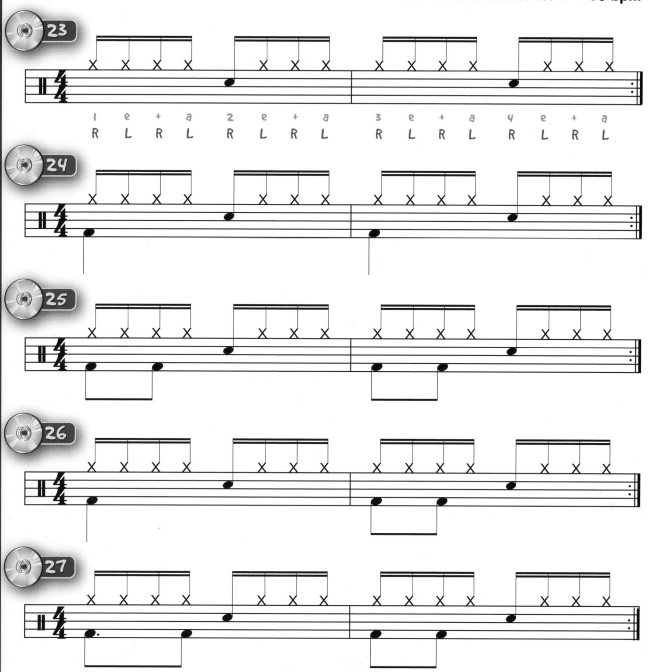

Blues Triplet Rhythms.

Here we have a chance to **s-l-o-w d-o-w-n** and concentrate on **'the blues'**.
Also this will be the first time that we look at **triplet timing**.
Exercises 29 and 32 are used in **'Swinging Blues'** on page 11.
For fun try **exercises 28, 30 and 31** with the backing track on the CD
to improve your improvisation.

Set the metronome to: ♩ = 60 bpm

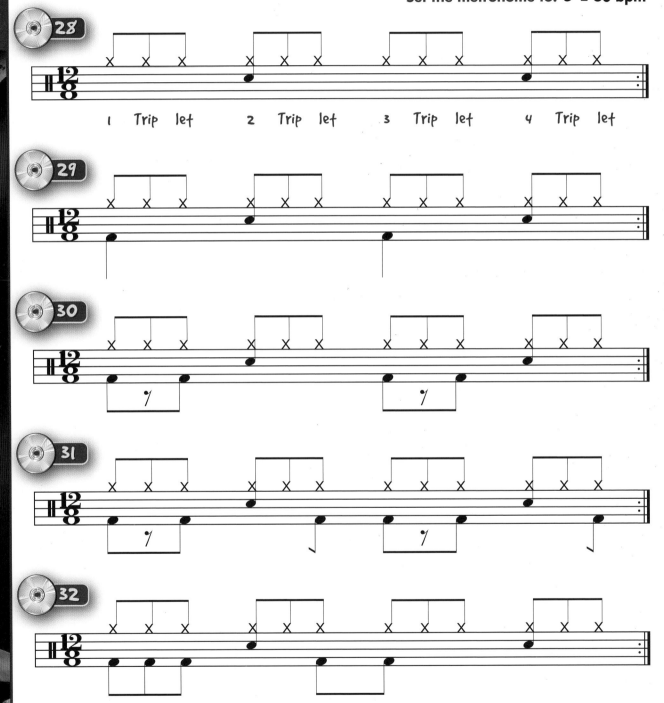

Swinging blues.

metronome
60
setting

33 + 34

Set the metronome to: ♩ = 60 bpm

POP

Pop.

Session 16

We now come back to the pop style and introduce **2 bar rhythms.** We have carefully chosen the rhythms to **mix 'n match**. Try taking any of the following samples below and place them into any order you wish.

Bar 1 exercise 35 and **bar 2 exercise 36**   **Bar 2 exercise 35** and **bar 1 exercise 36**
Bar 1 exercise 35 and **bar 2 exercise 37**   **Bar 2 exercise 35** and **bar 1 exercise 38**
Bar 1 exercise 35 and **bar 1 exercise 39**   **Bar 1 exercise 35** and **bar 2 exercise 40**

There are 1000,s of combinations...

Set the metronome to: ♩ = 80 bpm

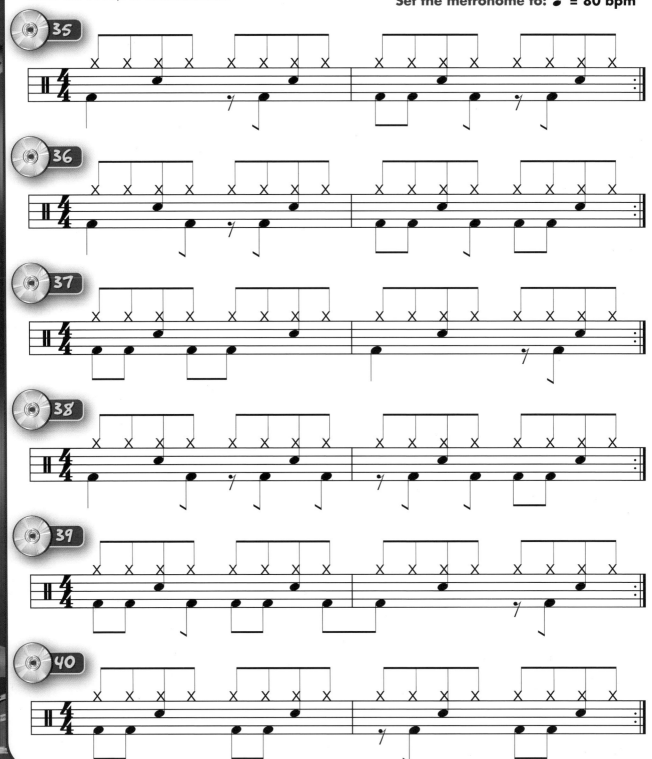

©2005 by Southern Counties Music Publishing. Photocopying is illegal.

12

High hat open.

This will be the first time we have seen a **high hat *open***. Try not to leave the high hat open too long as it will mix into the more defined beats and sound **muddy!**

Exercise 41 takes a **basic pop rhythm** from **Trainer book 1** and the **high hat opens** on the **4+**.

Exercise 42 takes the high hat **open** on the **2nd beat**.

Exercise 43 is on all the **off beats** and creates a ***disco style beat.***

Set the metronome to: ♩ = 80 bpm

BUILDING A BEAT

You should carefully **build** each section and only **move on** once you have **mastered** each part. If you do not take this approach your **beat will break down.** Once achieved you will have completed your **first fully coordinated rhythm** with *all four limbs!*

Set the metronome to: ♩ = 80 bpm

44 Here we start with the **basic** pop beat.

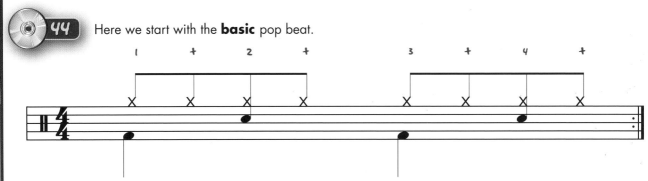

45 Then we add our **first crash cymbal** on beat 1.

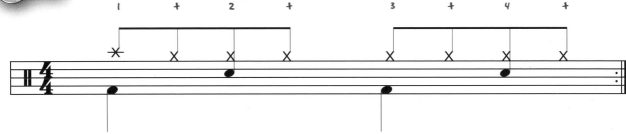

46 Now we have moved the **right hand** onto the **ride** and your **left foot** onto the **high hat.**

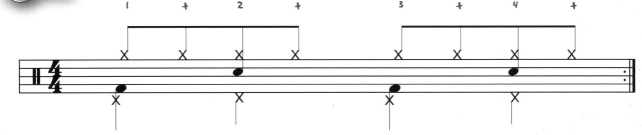

47 Finally we put the **crash cymbal** back in on beat 1.

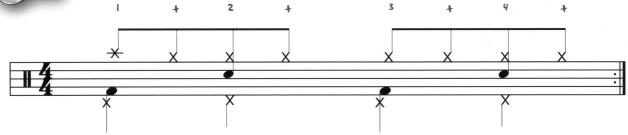

Fills.

metronome
100
setting

Fills are very important. As well as playing very **tight beats** they keep the **pulse** within the band. They are often **lead points** for changes to **middle 8, verses, choruses and solos.**

Try playing **exercises 48 – 51.** Once you understand the concept, try making up your own **2nd bar fill** in the space provided below.

Set the metronome to: ♩ = **100 bpm**

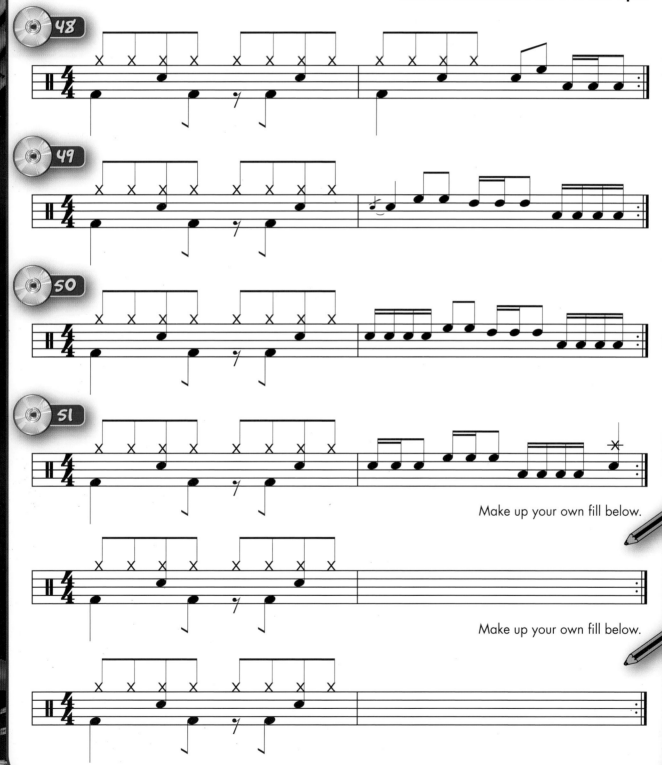

Make up your own fill below.

Make up your own fill below.

Madness Mania.

Session 20

Set the metronome to: ♩ = 100 bpm

52 + 53

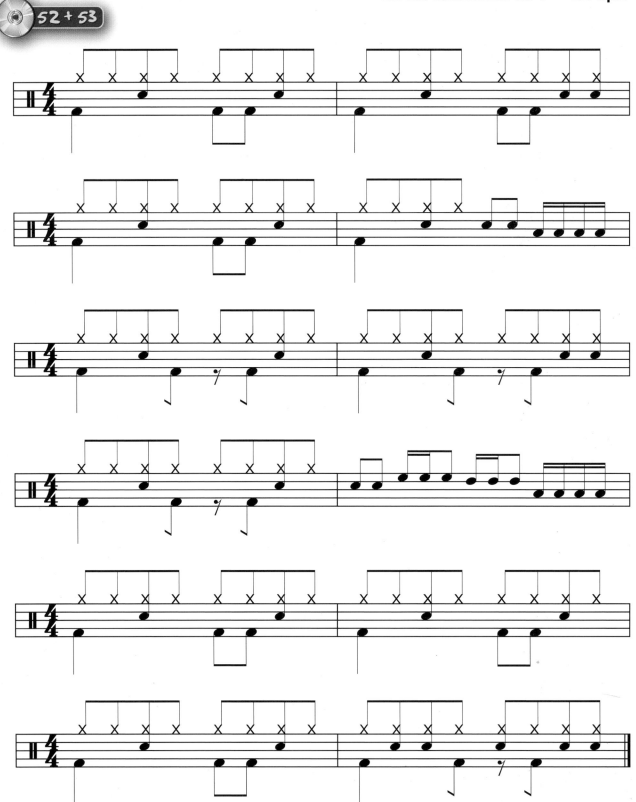

Congratulations.

You have now completed Drum Trainer Book 2!

Drum Trainer
BOOK 2

This is to certify that

_____
STUDENT NAME

has successfully completed

Drum Trainer
BOOK 2

_____
COACH

_____
SIGNATURE OF COACH

_____
DATE ACCOMPLISHED

_____
AWARD ACHIEVED

_____
MEDAL PRESENTED

SCAMPS

RAISING THE STANDARDS IN MUSIC EDUCATION